# THE LANGUAGE OF LOVE

# THE LANGUAGE OF Love

A Romantic Miscellany

Robyn Officer

ARIEL BOOKS

**Andrews McMeel Publishing**

Kansas City

 For information write Andrews McMeel Publishing, an Andrews McMeel Universal company, 4520 Main Street, Kansas City, Missouri 64111.

ISBN: 0-7407-2216-6
Library of Congress Catalog Card Number: 2003100781

LOVE
LOVE
LOVE
LOVE

LOVE

The symbols of Love—flowers, fragrance, singing birds, pounding hearts—are timeless and universal. This book is filled with famous words that brought these classic symbols to dazzling life, as well as with the messages of love that certain flowers convey.

All of the beau-tiful imagery is

complemented by
the pastoral charm
of Robyn Officer's
illustrations. Keep
this lovely book close
to your heart and
steep yourself in the
knowledge of romance!

That Love
is
all there is,

Is all we
know
of Love.

—Emily Dickinson

# How do I love thee?

Let me count
the ways.
I love thee to
the depth and
breadth and
height my
soul can reach....

I love thee with the
breath, smiles, tears
of all my life!
—and, if God choose,
I shall love thee
better after death.

—Elizabeth Barrett Browning

# Flowers of Love...

L·O·V·E

O, my Luve is like
a red, red rose
That's newly sprung
in June.
O, my Luve is like
the melodie
That's sweetly played
in tune.

—Robert Burns

LOVE doesn't make the world go 'round. LOVE is what makes the ride worthwhile.

—Franklin P. Jones

Place a pea pod with nine peas

in it under your kitchen door. The next person to come in—or someone with the same name as that person—will be your true love.

Flowers of Love...

# FAITHFULNESS

Doubt that the stars
are fire;
Doubt that the sun
doth move;
Doubt truth to
be a liar;
But never doubt
I love.

—William Shakespeare

Find the seed at the bottom of your heart and bring forth a flower.

—Shigenori Kameoka

She is a winsome wee thing,
She is a handsome wee thing,
She is a lo'e some wee thing,
This sweet wee wife o' mine.

—Robert Burns

# Flowers of Love...

I love you.
And it's getting worse.

—Joseph Morris

Love comforteth like sunshine after rain.
William Shakespeare

Earth's crammed with heaven

—Elizabeth Barrett Browning

Flowers of Love...

# Constancy

Grow old
along with me!
The best is yet to be,
the last of life,
for which the first
was made.

—Robert Browning

You
must always
be
A-WAGGLE
with love.

—D. H. Lawrence

Catch a ladybug, then let it fly away. It will invariably fly in the direction of your true love.

L·O·V·E

is or it ain't.

THIN LOVE

ain't love at all.

—Toni Morrison

Love is a little haven of refuge from the world.
Bertrand Russell

Flowers of Love...

# JOY

## Gardenia

When
you love someone
all your saved-up
wishes
start coming
out.

—Elizabeth Bowen

I love you
as New Englanders love

—Don Marquis

Nobody has ever measured, not even poets, how much the

HEART

can hold.

—Zelda Fitzgerald

If ever two
were one, then surely we.
If ever man were loved
by wife,
then thee...

—Anne Bradstreet

Name an apple seed or nut after your love and place it in a fire. If it pops, you are loved; if it burns without a sound, your lover cares little.

Flowers of Love...

There is no fear
in love;
but perfect love
casteth out
fear.

—I John 4:18

WE LOVE BEING IN LOVE, THAT'S *the* TRUTH ON'T.

—William Makepeace Thackeray

LOVE is AN IRRESISTIBLE DESIRE TO BE IRRESISTIBLY DESIRED.

—Robert Frost

LOVE

makes
hard hearts
gentle.

—Proverb

Two souls but a single thought,
Two hearts that beat as one.
—Von Munch-Bellinghausen

Flowers of Love...

# Daisy

## Mutual feelings

Love does not
consist in
gazing at each other
but in looking
together
in the same
direction.

—Antoine de Saint-Exupéry

When the one man
loves the one woman
and the one woman
loves the one man,
the very angels leave
heaven and come and
sit in that house and
sing for joy.

—Brahma

# LOVE

is such a funny thing; It's very like a lizard; It twines itself around your heart And penetrates your gizzard. . . .

—Anonymous

Tomatoes, once called "love apples," were considered so powerful an aphrodisiac that Puritans were not allowed to even put them on the dinner table.

# Flowers of Love...

Love is like a
beautiful flower
which I may not
touch, but whose
fragrance makes
the garden a place
of delight just
the same.

—Helen Keller

IF YOU WOULD BE LOVED, LOVE AND BE LOVABLE.

—Benjamin Franklin

True love never grows old.

—Proverb

I love you,

NOT ONLY FOR

WHAT YOU ARE,

BUT

for what I am

WHEN I AM WITH

YOU.

—Roy Croft

Honey, known as the "nectar of the gods," with its thick, sensual sweetness, has long been a food of love.

Flowers of Love...

Bachelor's Button

HOPE

Whoso
LOVES
believes
the
impossible.

—Elizabeth Barrett Browning

The heart that loves is forever young.

—Greek proverb

Love doesn't just sit there like a stone; it has to be made, like bread; remade all the time, made new.

—Ursula K. LeGuin

*Flowers of Love...*

# Happiness

Lily of the Valley

Breathless,
we flung us
on the windy hill,
Laughed
in the sun,
and kissed the
lovely grass.

—Rupert Brooke

There is nothing holier,

in this life of ours,
than the
first consciousness
of love— the first
fluttering of its silken
wings.

—Henry Wadsworth Longfellow

A life without love is like a year without SUMMER.

—Swedish proverb